Apples Rot on the Ground

poems by

Kate Padilla

Finishing Line Press
Georgetown, Kentucky

Apples Rot
on the Ground

Copyright © 2020 by Kate Padilla
ISBN 978-1-64662-193-4 First Edition
All rights reserved under International and Pan-American Copyright Conventions. No part of this book may be reproduced in any manner whatsoever without written permission from the publisher, except in the case of brief quotations embodied in critical articles and reviews.

ACKNOWLEDGMENTS

"BITCH" appeared in *Hers, A Poets Speak Anthology, Fix & Free Anthology & Rolling Sixes Sestinas.*
"VANISHING HISTORY" is a Pushcart nominee, appeared in *Weaving the Terrain* and *Fix & Free Anthology 2018.*
"MY NAME IS PADILLA" and "THE RUSTLER" appeared in *Weavin'2*
"EL VATO AND THE BEES" is a third place winner by Southwest Writers, appeared in *Pudding Magazine.*
"SCHOOL YARD GANGLAND" appeared in *Adobe Walls Anthology* and *Poetry from the Other Side.*
"TAOS HARVEST" appeared in *Rolling Sixes Sestinas* and *Water, A Poets Speak Anthology.*

Publisher: Leah Maines
Editor: Christen Kincaid
Cover Art: Kate Padilla
Author Photo: Jerry Redfern
Cover Design: Elizabeth Maines McCleavy

Printed in the USA on acid-free paper.
Order online: www.finishinglinepress.com
also available on amazon.com

Author inquiries and mail orders:
Finishing Line Press
P. O. Box 1626
Georgetown, Kentucky 40324
U. S. A.

Table of Contents

Bitch (sestina) 1

Vanishing History 3

My Name Is Padilla 4

First Memory 5

Rustler 6

Forbidden Friend 7

School Yard Gangland 1950 8

Winters 9

Nothing to be Thankful For 10

Alonzo the Shoeshine Boy (pantoum) 11

El Vato and The Bees 12

Wyoming Neighborhood 13

Bath Day 14

A Santo Protects My Mother 15

Burial 16

Taos Harvest (sestina) 17

For my mother
Juana Margarita Martinez Padilla

BITCH

> *They say I'm a beast*
> *And feast on it. When all along*
> *I thought that's what a woman was.*
> *They say I'm a bitch.*
> *Or witch. I've claimed*
> *the same and never winced.*
> *—From "Loose Woman," Sandra Cisneros*

Let me holler like a beast
screech and pull along-
side those machos who say I was
nothing but a bitch,
but I fisted up and claimed
my place in line. I didn't wince.

Años pasados, I witnessed a woman wince,
forced to kneel before the beast,
whose traditions sanctioned his claim
on her as if she were property along
with his horses and bitch
dogs. But we aren't what *we was*

back then, when my mother was
told when to breathe, and when she winced
afraid when he called her a bitch,
a word he learned from other beasts,
macho men who went along
denying their wives' claim

for space where peace is claimed,
a safe place. She was
a trusting woman until he came along.
At first it was love, then she winced
after marriage when the jealous beast
struck her for being rich

in beauty and intelligence. From them a bitch
was born, a daughter who disputed claims
and customs, who stood against the beast,
embraced her mother who was
until her death afraid. She winced
at his presence, unable to challenge the long-

forged family norms of long-
ago. She was *nada*, never a bitch
who could make the tribe wince.
Her well-armored daughter claimed
her own voice. In her determination she was
fearless, prepared to take down the beast.

The daughter didn't wince. She stretched a long
rope and baited the beast, yelled, "I am a bitch."
Claimed the podium. She was not her mother, afraid.

VANISHING HISTORY

My great-grandmother is buried
in Arroyo Seco

As is my grandmother

My mother was birthed
in this same New Mexico village

I was born nearby in Taos
That is all I know

Aunt Bessie is 91
my last link to bygone days

I beg her for stories

We walk behind
the family adobe home

She plucks plums off
the trees planted
ages ago

She complains bears eat her apples

I beg her for stories

She unbuttons her blouse
asks me to touch her breast
the lump a steely marble

She shows me her last
three pots of porch geraniums

MY NAME IS PADILLA

Inspired by Martín Espada's poem, "My Name is Espada."

Padilla soldiers rode out of Spain
in armor and in helmets embellished
with feathers resplendent of quetzals.
Padillas' coats-of-arms, a war-cry,
fingers gripped sabers meant to colonize.

They spilled Aztec blood, raped women,
their blood mixed in veins birthing children
with sculpted high cheek bones.
They traveled the Camino Real in New Mexico
to confiscate Native tribal lands.

In the San Luis Valley, my grandfather's illusions
of grandeur dissolved, his Jewish heritage
secreted in trunks. My father denied his Mexican
ancestry, identified himself as Spanish-American.

Martinez, my mother's clan are farmers—
their emblem is Mars, the fertility God.
Martinez were born under trees and stars,
joyous when squash vines coiled
up string beans against mud walls.

Martinez found joy when snowflakes mounded
on Blue Mountain, and melted into the Rio Grande.
Martinez women were *curanderas* and midwives,
Martinez women never cut their hair.

Today, Padillas carry virtual swords to cliff tops,
fight with words and gamble with life.
My name is Padilla and I am a poet with a mean streak
yet I am joyous when I see my string beans wrap
around my corn stalks in New Mexico where I was born.

FIRST MEMORY

Hands lifted my asleep body
red flames ate our home

Snow on the ground

Hands blanketed me
carried me into an away dream
set me down atop a rosy-lit kitchen counter

Woman with a foreign voice
tenderly tapped my knee
she swayed toward a white door

I see bright colored shapes inside

She hands me a sweet cold drink
my legs flutter with joy

RUSTLER

> *I went to the woods because I wanted to live deliberately, I wanted to live deep and suck out all the marrow of life ...* Henry David Thoreau

My mother stands at the living room window looking across the street toward the city jail. Her nostrils flare in anger like my grandfather's white stallion trapped in his stall. This morning before dawn my father packed his green panel truck with winter coats he bought at garage sales, boxes of glazed donuts, cans of fruit cocktail and several bottles of whiskey. He drove into the Wyoming desert toward the sheepherders' camp. He had spotted it last week when he and my mother drove down Highway 30 to the shopping mall in the next town. When my father saw smoke rising over distant sagebrush-spattered hills, like a gambler who spys an old flame, he ached for his pastoral threads. He knew sheepherding. He was sixteen when he tended sheep in the Medicine Bow Mountains. He remembered the aloneness, howling coyotes, winter nights under rough woolen quilts listening to the overhead canvas thrashing against the sheep wagon. He loved his horse and dogs most. As he drove toward the camp, my father knew the herders would speak Spanish and they would welcome kin. The two herders and my father sat on camp steps viewing the Red Desert, they drank whiskey-spiked coffee while rabbit stew cooked on the potbelly stove. My father told sheepherding stories of the day when his horse saved his life in a blinding snow storm and of the night his partner died from tick fever. My father's visit was rewarded with a fresh-killed lamb, just as my mother feared. Cold afternoon shadows etched harsh lines on her worried face, certain my father would be arrested for rustling by the ranch *patron*, who owned the herd. In Wyoming the penalty was jail time. Hours after sunset, we heard the crunching sound of gravel as my father backed his truck into the homemade garage where he would butcher the gifted mutton. My mother collapsed into a chair. That evening my father and I chomped on the just-cooked ribs and lamb chops. Grease dripped down my face, my brown cheeks aglow as my fingers plowed into bones and sucked out the treasured marrow.

FORBIDDEN FRIEND

Charlie Ray Davis swings high—
freckle face, carrot hair, rice paper skin.
His blood pumps so fast I fear his veins
will burst and he'll bleed to death.

I am a shy eight-year-old brown girl,
bony knees, ribbons securing ends
of long black braids that fly
when it's my turn on the swing.

After school we grab hands, play rope.
He pulls, twists me fast around the corner.
I fall, he laughs and helps me up.
Then it's my turn.

I twist, pull him all the way home,
down to our apartment building,
long and narrow, set on top
of the old veterans' cemetery.

At the back door his mother stands guard.
She hollers, *Charlie! Charlie Ray Davis*
get your ass away
from that dirty Mexican!

At the clothesline hanging laundry,
my mother twists her neck ugly.
She screams, *Katalina! I've told you before,*
stay away from that white trash Okie!

SCHOOLYARD GANGLAND 1950

Wyoming wind rages
into our railroad shack—
coal ash coats,
plates of beans and tortillas.

We tremble
in our family's
steel bed
with passing trains.

Wyoming wind sucks
cigarette smoke
from the circle
of five *Chicanas*.

We control
the furthest corner
of the junior
high campus.

Wyoming wind gusts
scream open our blue
nylon windbreakers
like angel wings.

We finger brass knuckles,
push forward
over dry aspen leaves,
power in our pockets.

WINTERS

New Mexico nights
meant wood fires
in metal stove.

Adobe home held
warmth until morning.

Nights in Wyoming
meant gas heater.

My father feared the pilot light
would burst into flames
and burn down our frame house.

Nights were cold.

My brother Balta
shared his covers.

A warm memory
of a brother killed
in a car rollover.

"NOTHING TO BE THANKFUL FOR"

There was never a question
who would get my father's saxophone.
Balta was my father's favorite.
Girls couldn't blow hard enough
to make music.

When Balta knocked up
his 16-year-old girlfriend,
my stern Chicano father cried.
He offered him money to run away.

My brother married her anyway,
left college and found a construction job
at the Flaming Gorge Dam
miles away from home.

Worried for his pregnant wife
he drove the short-cut home.
Only the moon saw the car roll.
His tear-stained face
scraped the wet dirt road.

My father wailed.
My mother fell into a silent space.
I was locked out of their pain.

Thanksgiving weekend
I was left without homemade pumpkin pies,
empanadas with pine nuts.
I missed my father mixing highballs,
my mother wearing lipstick.

We were flushed down a love-deprived vortex.
I married a stranger who promised me
a holiday with all the trimmings.
My father sought sexual comfort elsewhere.
My mother stuffed her wedding dress
into the alley trash can and lit a match.

ALONZO THE SHOESHINE BOY

A shoeshine boy walks over the viaduct
in his hand a wooden shoeshine box
with a knife-whittled-foot sized for soldiers
new recruits at Warren Air Force base

In his hand a wooden shoeshine box
stocked with black and brown KIWI tins
for new recruits at Warren Air Force base
soldiers ready to shell out dimes for a spit shine

Stocked with black and brown KIWI tins
the boy buffs boots with a slapping flannel cloth
for soldiers ready to shell out dimes for a spit shine
money for the boy to buy cigarettes and pomade

The boy buffs boots with a slapping flannel cloth
a final whack with his father's bristle brush earns
the boy money to buy cigarettes and pomade
for his ducktail and comic books to trade

A final whack with his father's bristle brush earns
praise for his rebel streak soldiers' tips
for his ducktail and comic books to trade
on the corner where his ego struts

In pockets full of ready money scored
with a knife-whittled-foot sized for soldiers
a prize held tight by darkened fingers at dusk
a shoeshine boy walks over the viaduct

EL VATO AND THE BEES

A ballet etched in my child's mind.

A summer day in Taos shattered
by a chilling chorus of screams
angry bees buzzing attacking
round my grandfather's bald head
like a spiked halo.

He stumbles, a lone strap from his coveralls
drifts off his shoulder to the ground.
His frantic arms swing at the stinging bees,
red terror fills his wet wide open eyes,
he drops face down.

My grandmother pulls a *serape*
off the bed and chases out the adobe house.
She drags grandfather under the cloak.
Like a giant ladybug they move slowly
away from the tormented bees.

Alonzo is a *vato*, hair slicked back like Elvis,
his arms lined with welts from my father's belt.
His sinful face hides behind the apple tree.

My grandfather and his father and his father
use marijuana smoke to calm the bees.
Today my grandfather's bellows smoker
is filled with dry tree leaves.

Alonzo's lust for marijuana turns
today's honey harvest ghastly.

WYOMING NEIGHBORHOOD

My father in anger speed
chases down onto the street

He yanks up my brother's Levis

Alonzo is a want-to-be *Pachuco*
his fashion style threatens
my father's get-along stance

Alonzo rolls forbidden cigarettes
in white T-shirt sleeves

He is sixteen

My father moves quietly
speaks Spanish only
behind closed window blinds

Alonzo won't isolate himself
a bully with pomaded black hair
combed into a duck tail

His disguise conceals
frightened brown nakedness

He breaks free
struts round the block
shoves his jeans back down
below his waist

A chain dangles

BATH DAY

The clouds cold in Wyoming
float south to New Mexico
where I am safe from bigotry—
a strange word for a six-year-old.
It hurts just the same. I am not
a "dirty Mexican" in my grandma's
adobe home that smells of anise.

When sun rises over Blue Mountain
she coils her long gray hair into a bun.
She hauls buckets of well water
to heat in a wood stove
for my Saturday bath in a metal tub.

A smiling moment with sunshine
pouring through the window.
Her calloused hands washing my hair
I am secure in the smell of her armpits.

She sits me on a stool
wrapped in a towel to dry
while she reuses my bath water
to wet down dirt floors
pours what is left on her flowers.

This memory is my shield against
Wyoming's racist arrows cast against
my brown skin with the burning message
"Dirty Mexican. Go Home."

A SANTO PROTECTS MY MOTHER

Lean and wasted
she takes away the loaded
gun pointed at his head.

Together my mother
and father leave
the women's shelter.

In Espanola I bought my parents
a picture of Santo Nino de Atocha
glued onto a piece of tin.

Tiny broken red pieces
of glass framed the
protector of prisoners.

He rides on the dashboard
of my father's car.

BURIAL

Wet shovels of sand
closed up my father's
painful cancer. His
coffin—gold, gilded
like my mother's.

I grip the blurred,
blown-up photo.
His face stern at 93
stares back at me.

His eyes key
to the vaulted secrets
of machismo.

TAOS HARVEST

On a wooden table sit loaves of warm bread,
adobe house heated with firewood,
air smells of yeast and burned bark from a cedar tree.
It is August, apples rotting on the ground
so many trees bearing fruit,
acequias overflowing. Oh, sweet water

gifted down from Blue Lake. Sacred water
mixed into flour for today's Indian bread.
Extra dough rolled, spooned-in fruit
for empanadas, baked in mud ovens with firewood.
Up the Rio Grande, foreigners prepare ground
to divert our water and claim our trees.

White laws say we no longer can cut trees.
Manmade dams have cut off the floodwaters
our families need to soak sacred ground
where we harvest wheat to make our bread.
Locked gates deny access to firewood.
Our wagons return to the pueblo empty. Fruit

no longer in abundance. Oh, we remember sweet fruit,
flowers budding, beehives in the trees,
trips up the mountain for firewood,
how we cupped our hands to drink water
from the stream, how we shared bread,
how we danced upon our ancient ground.

Our ancestors tell us to stand our ground,
remind us wind, land, water are fruit
for all to share, to honor life-giving bread.
We dance and pray under the trees
call upon the gods to return our water.
In our sacred circle we burn firewood.

A gold flame fed by our firewood
like the morning sun tipping the ground
we identify our path to save our water,
to bring back to the pueblo people. Fruit
will again fall off the trees.
We will harvest corn for our bread.

We will persevere, our water will again flow, our firewood
will burn to bake our bread, our sacred ground
will award us a richness, trees laden with fruit.

Kate Padilla's edgy writings recall her Taos birthplace, and growing up in conservative Wyoming, where her parents had relocated for work.

She's bilingual, a University of Wyoming graduate, worked as a journalist in both radio and print, and subsequently became a U.S. senator's aide in Washington, D.C. Padilla transferred to the federal Bureau of Land Management, first, as an environmental planner, and then as Field Manager in Socorro, New Mexico, for seven years until her retirement in 2005.

While in Socorro as a manager, Padilla was a key player in developing the unique Camino Real International Heritage Center in central New Mexico that tells the history of the Mexicans, Spanish, Anglos, and Native Americans who traveled for centuries along as El Camino Real Terra de Adentro. She also taught in Spanish the principals of Environmental Assessment to the Tarahumara Indians in Mexico

Padilla has studied creative writing at the University of New Mexico, reviews books for Authorlink.com, and in 2017 she was a Pushcart nominee from New Mexico for her poetry.

Over the past 30 years, she and spouse Paul Krza have periodically traveled, on unplanned and unexpected journeys, to places like Gjirokastër, Albania; Sofia, Bulgaria; Ho Chi Minh City, Vietnam, and Havana, Cuba. She's also spent considerable time in Ljubljana, Slovenia, where her spouse recently gained citizenship.

www.ingramcontent.com/pod-product-compliance
Lightning Source LLC
LaVergne TN
LVHW041525070426
835507LV00013B/1823